BREEDERS' BEST®
A KENNEL CLUB BOOK®

Siberian Husky

By Kathleen Kanzler

D0921937

3/05
Sue

BREEDERS' BEST®
A KENNEL CLUB BOOK®

SIBERIAN HUSKY

ISBN: 1-59378-920-6

Copyright © 2004

Kennel Club Books, LLC
308 Main Street, Allenhurst, NJ 07711 USA
Printed in South Korea

PHOTOS BY:
Isabelle Français,
Carol Ann Johnson
and Bernd Brinkmann.

DRAWINGS BY:
Yolyanko el Habanero

Contents

CHAPTER 1

Meet the Siberian Husky

The history of the Siberian Husky is filled with high drama and adventure. Unlike other canids that evolved over the centuries on the plains of Europe and later crossed the Atlantic Ocean, the Husky was and still remains a purely Nordic breed of dog. He was developed in north-eastern Asia by the Siberian tribe of Chukchi Indians as a sled dog, their primary means of transportation. The tribesmen bred the dogs for endurance, using them for transport to better hunting grounds, traveling long distances over ice and snow. The Chukchi's revered their canine workers and treated them like

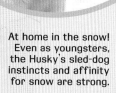

At home in the snow! Even as youngsters, the Husky's sled-dog instincts and affinity for snow are strong.

family members. The dogs had delightful temperaments, lived in the family shelters and played happily with the Chukchi children. That engaging temperament is still present in the 21st-century Siberian Husky.

Sled-dog races are still held, primarily in Alaska, the largest and most famous of which is the Iditarod, covering 1,200 miles of frozen terrain.

The Husky's first known migration onto North American soil occurred in 1909 when Russian fur trader, William Goosak imported a team of Siberians, known then as the Siberian dog, to Nome, Alaska. Goosak entered his dogs in the 408-mile All-Alaska Sweepstakes race, hoping to capture the $10,000 purse offered to the winning team. His team was dismissed as lightweights who were no match for their taller, heavier competitors. In a surprise finish, Goosak's team took third place, and their strong showing impressed the other racers. The little dogs' reputation spread rapidly across the continent.

Backpacking is a favorite activity for Huskies and owners living in more temperate climes.

Based on their 1909 performance, three Siberian teams were entered the following year in the next All-Alaska race. The three teams placed first, second and fourth, with the winning team setting a race record that remained unbroken for the next seven years. It is no surprise that the small but mighty Siberian had earned the respect and admiration of the people of Alaska.

In 1925, the Siberian Husky embarked on the historic Serum Run, the life-saving mission across Alaska that launched the breed into the public eye. The city of Nome was paralyzed by a diphtheria epidemic, and the closest lifesaving serum was 600 miles away in the City of Neana. Sled-dog trainer and racer, Leonhard Seppala volunteered his Siberians, who were descendants of the original imports from Siberia. Seppala drove his team of 20 dogs, led by his leader dog,

Togo, through blizzard conditions across 300 miles of perilous terrain, to meet the relay team carrying the medicine. Tired and worn, Seppala's team then turned back toward Nome. A second team, led by the great Siberian, Balto, completed the last leg of the journey and delivered the serum. Both lead dogs, Togo and Balto, were honored for their valor. A statue of Balto stands in New York's Central Park in memory of all of the dogs that participated in the Serum Run.

Buoyed by his team's success, Seppala entered his Siberians in several New England races, pitting them against the favored locally bred racing dogs. The Siberians consistently bested the bigger dogs, and Seppala amassed more wins and records in that area than any other musher. His dogs were suddenly in great demand, and his kennel provided many fine Siberians to the New England mushers and kennels during the 1930s.

Those East Coast fanciers applied for and received American Kennel Club (AKC) differed. But the working Siberian was paramount, and show dogs often worked on the racing teams of their time. More than just a few great racers and leaders are found

The Siberian Husky has proven itself to be the fastest and most dependable sled-dog breed. A team of dogs in action is an amazing sight.

recognition for the breed in 1930. The Siberian Husky Club of America (SHCA) was founded eight years later in 1938.

There was little uniformity in the appearance of the early Siberian, with some long and leggy, and others shorter coupled and heavier boned, and markings that also in upfront generations of many Siberian Husky show dogs.

Due to the many generations of emphasis on performance as well as form, the urge to run and race is still prominent in the 21st-century Siberian Husky. The dual-purpose Husky is espoused by many prominent breeders who race their Siberians, some competing in the annual classic Iditarod Trail sled-dog race.

The Siberian Husky's gentle demeanor is no doubt a relic of its past, dating back to the adaptable and affectionate Husky who lived with the Chukchi tribes. However, his intelligence and independent streak also dominate his personality, which at times can challenge even the most astute of owners. But such versatility lends a charming and intriguing appeal to the Husky personality.

The Siberian is not

The Norwegian Elkhound is another of the Northern breeds, possessing many common traits with the Siberian Husky.

The Husky perhaps is most often mistaken for the larger Alaskan Malamute, shown here.

considered a one-person dog, and he shows his affection equally to all members of his family. He is interested in strangers and is unflinching and cordial when greeted by outsiders, but his propriety rules him out as a true guardian breed. However, his unusual brilliant eyes can be intimidating, and those unfamiliar with the breed may feel put off or threatened by the Husky's "icy" stare.

The Husky is also friendly and tolerant of strange dogs. If, however, he is attacked, he is a formidable adversary, ready and more than able to defend himself. While the Husky is gentle and amiable with other canines, he is not so with small animals such as cats, squirrels, rabbits and other typical house pets such as guinea pigs and hamsters. His predatory instincts remain strong, and he will not be deterred if he is on the hunt. All small creatures are considered prey and are great risk in a Husky household.

Siberian Husky puppies display all of the usual mischievous habits one associates with puppies. They are very active and energetic, they love to explore and chew for the sheer pleasure of doing so. They also have a special proclivity for digging, which is a self-rewarding behavior that can be difficult to control, much less eliminated entirely.

In terms of feeding, the Husky is not demanding and requires less food than most dogs his size, a quality of economy many find

The talents of the Siberian Husky can be utilized in other helpful ways. This pack is in training with a resourceful owner.

appealing. Breed historians speculate that this trait dates back to the Chukchis who honed their dogs into tenacious workers who could pull their sleds over great distances in very cold temperatures on a bare minimum of rations, thus reducing the need to add dog food to their sled load.

Perhaps the Siberian is most true to his ancestry in his desire to run. He has an insatiable passion for running, and run he will at every opportunity. For his own safety and well-being, the Husky should never be permitted to run free.

Despite the obvious challenges in owning a Siberian Husky, the breed ranks high in AKC annual registrations with around 12 to 15,000 dogs registered. Thanks to the dedicated efforts of breeders, sled-dog racing enthusiasts, exhibitors and other members of the SHCA, the modern Husky is one of the few breeds that has retained those original mental and physical qualities that make it a competent working dog an a devoted companion.

MEET THE SIBERIAN HUSKY

Overview

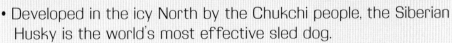

- Developed in the icy North by the Chukchi people, the Siberian Husky is the world's most effective sled dog.
- The Chukchi people lived with the Huskies and treated them as family members.
- William Goosak imported the first Huskies from Siberia in 1909. History records other famous events that led to the breed's being hailed as an exception working dog and handsome companion.
- The breed today is among the most versatile, affectionate and beautiful.

Description of the Husky

A breed standard attempts to paint a picture of the ideal dog of a particular breed, describing appearance, proper structure, and the function or purpose for which the dog was originally bred. Perhaps no standard does so better than that of the Siberian Husky. The Siberian is a working dog, a medium-sized athlete who was bred to work as a sled dog in harness. Every element in his standard is designed toward that end.

The Siberian Husky looks very much like the Northern wolves from which it descended.

The importance of function and performance is evident in "General Appearance," which is the first paragraph of the American Kennel Club (AKC) standard. "His characteristic gait is smooth and seemingly effortless. He performs his original function in harness most capably, carrying a light load at a moderate speed over great distances. His body proportions and form reflect this balance of power, speed and endurance." The framers of the original standard obviously intended to ensure that the descendants of the original working Husky retain those defining characteristics.

The Husky can have many different marking patterns; subtle differences create a wide range of possibilities in the breed.

The male Husky stands 21 to 23.5 inches at the withers and weighs 45 to 60 pounds; the female, 20 to 22 inches and weighs 35 to 50 pounds. Excessive bone or weight is to be penalized, and oversize by even half an inch is a disqualification. Such rigid guidelines place further emphasis on the importance of

Physical condition is of utmost importance in a breed designed for endurance. The body must be muscular and fit, with sound bone and strong, straight legs.

proper working form.

The Husky is described as "well-furred." He carries a double coat of medium length, with a soft, dense undercoat that supports the smooth guard hairs of the outer coat. The standard penalizes any trimming of any part of the coat, other than to tidy the fur between the toes and around the feet. With no trimming necessary,

The Husky is not a longhaired breed, but rather a densely coated breed. His double coat serves to protect him from the elements, keeping him insulated and repelling snow and other moisture.

the Husky is thus considered an "easy keeper," although many would dispute that during those times when the

Husky sheds his very profuse undercoat.

Coat colors from black to pure white are acceptable. A variety of markings on the head is common, including many striking patterns which are not found in other breeds. Some of these patterns give the pure-bred Husky a rather "wild look," befitting his close relation to the wolf.

The tail is also furry from top to bottom and gives the appearance of a round brush. It curves over the back in a graceful sickle arc when the dog is at attention, and trails downward when in repose. It should not curl to either side of the body or snap flat against the back.

The Husky's eyes are one of his most unique features, one for which he is often remembered. They are almond shaped and a tad oblique, or slanted upward. Blue and brown are acceptable colors. His ears are triangular in shape, thick and furry. Set high on his head, they should be "strongly" erect and pointing straight up.

Husky temperament is of paramount importance. He should be friendly and gentle, but also alert and outgoing. The Husky does not display the possessive qualities of the guard dog, nor is he overly suspicious of strangers or aggressive with other dogs. Some measure of reserve and dignity may be expected in the mature dog. His intelligence, tractability and eager disposition make him an agreeable companion and willing worker. His expression reflects those elements of his personality: keen, friendly, interested and even mischievous.

Since the original standard was first accepted by the AKC in 1932, it has survived five revisions, culminating in the current version. Such in-depth study indicates the dedication and commitment of breed fanciers to the dual-purpose Siberian Husky.

A DESCRIPTION OF THE HUSKY

Overview

- Adopted by the American Kennel Club, the breed standard describes the ideal Siberian Husky, as envisioned by the parent club.
- A breed standard details the dog's physical form as well as character and movement (called gait).
- The Husky stands between 20 and 23.5 inches and weighs 35 to 50 pounds.
- The breed's celebrated double coat is of medium length with a dense undercoat. Colors range from black to white.
- The Husky's almond-shaped eyes are obliquely slanted; the ears are small and triangular; the tail is well furred, curving in a sickle arch.

CHAPTER

Are You a Husky Person?

I t has been said that you can take the Husky out of Siberia, but you can't take Siberia out of the Husky. This is more than just a cold-weather dog. The Husky is a workhorse driven by a work ethic born of generations of sled dogs who pulled and raced under the direst of conditions. He is not satisfied with a life of unemployment. Without a job or challenge, the Husky will expend his energy in creatively destructive ways. He will dig beneath the largest rock, shinny under the strongest fence, and otherwise tax his owner's imagi-

"On the go" aptly describes the Husky puppy, and his energy level stays high throughout his life. Only owners seeking active companions should consider the Husky.

nation. Boredom is simply not in the Siberian's vocabulary.

That free spirit is a part of the Husky's charm and one of the unique qualities that draws many people to the breed. He is highly intelligent, but not easily trained, presenting both a challenge and conundrum. Consequently, the Husky requires an equally unique owner who is up to dealing with and enjoying the many facets of his personality. If you fancy a dog with a retriever's desire to please, a dog with guard-dog loyalty, or a dog that is half couch potato and content with solitude, the Husky is not the breed for you.

Outdoors, in the snow, with their owner—what more could this handsome pair ask for?

Despite his willful ways, the Siberian Husky is an affectionate and gregarious dog who needs to be with his person or family and does not thrive if left alone. He has a delightful temperament and relishes every opportunity to interact with people, young and old.

If you're looking for a dog who will jump for joy whenever he sees you, then the Husky might just be the dog for you.

He especially enjoys the company of young children and is most gentle and sweet tempered when playing with them.

A truly hospitable fellow, the Husky is not a guard or watchdog. He is friendly with strangers as well as family, although strangers often are intimidated by the Husky's appearance, especially his gleaming, wolf-like eyes.

The Siberian is equally pleasant with other dogs, having been for generations a sled-dog team player. Not so, however, with other small animals such as cats, rabbits or guinea pigs. His predatory instincts remain strong, and this normally gentle dog morphs into a swift and cunning hunter of small and hapless creatures. The Husky will not cohabit well with such small pets.

The Siberian coat is more evidence of his Arctic heritage. His fur is thick and plush, with a dense undercoat, which he sheds twice a year, sending clouds of downy fur throughout the house. If you are a fastidious housekeeper, think twice about living with a Husky. On the plus side, the heavy undercoat provides insulation from many of the skin allergens that irritate humans and keeps the dog relatively odor-free. Regular grooming, brushing and

Husky owners admit to being swept off their feet by this marvelous breed—and the feeling is mutual!

bathing, are most time-consuming but essential for healthy skin and coat.

Although the Husky is a medium-size dog, standing about 24 inches tall, he

your Husky will soon make short work of it.

His natural proclivity to run is perhaps the Husky's most dangerous shortcoming. He runs for the pure pleasure

The Husky's love of children is deeply ingrained in the breed, as they were raised with the Chukchi kids and were considered true members of the family. Nonetheless, all children should be taught how to handle the Husky properly and treat the dog with care and respect.

requires big-dog accommodations. A large yard is best to provide adequate exercise space, and a secure fence at least 5 feet high is a must. Huskies are quintessential diggers and runners who are relentlessly determined to do both. If you fancy a manicured, landscaped yard,

of doing what he was bred to do, a trait that must be controlled for his own safety. The Husky does not perceive the possible danger of an oncoming snowmobile or truck. Siberians must be housed and exercised in safely and securely enclosed areas, always exercised on leash or harness, and never permitted to run free. Simply stated, Siberian owners who allow otherwise put their dogs in harm's way and risk the loss of their dog to death or disappearance.

The Husky is best suited

each day. Long, brisk walks, swimming and sled-pulling events are excellent outlets for that boundless Husky energy.

Husky rescue groups, comprised of volunteers who dedicate themselves to finding homes for abandoned

Not just sled dogs, Huskies are versatile, fun-loving companions who delight in sharing whatever their owners do. This exuberant pair is helping their owner with his boat, looking forward to a day on the water.

for an active family who pursues activities that include their dog. He needs at least one hour of vigorous exercise

Siberian Huskies, believe that many owners are unprepared for the breed's high energy level, devilish mischief and other hard-to-handle traits. Many Huskies are abandoned because of behavior problems, and rescue groups attempt to rehome many of those dogs every year.

If you fancy living with a Siberian Husky, patronize only a knowledgeable breeder who will educate you about both sides of this intriguing breed. A responsible, caring breeder will be happy counsel you during all of the stages of the dog's development—and that's a good thing.

As true pack dogs, Huskies do well in multi-pet households and enjoy the company of other canines. This Husky and his Golden Retriever buddy are ready to hit the road!

ARE YOU A HUSKY PERSON?

Overview

- The Husky person relishes an active, outgoing dog that wants to become a member of his owner's pack.
- One of the Husky's most prized assets is his temperament, gregarious with other dogs and friendly toward people. Huskies make friends easily and happily.
- The well-furred Husky sheds coat around the house, and his wise, tidy owner keeps him brushed and doesn't mind a minor fur cloud under the coffee table.
- The Husky person lives in a home with a spacious yard and a trustworthy fence, keeping his ever-running Husky at home and safe. He is exercised on lead or in a safely confined area.

Selecting a Husky Breeder

Selecting a reputable breeder for the Siberian Husky is more important than it is for many other breeds. The Husky is a brilliant but challenging dog, and a knowledgeable breeder can explain the complexities of this intriguing animal so you can properly raise a Husky pup. Your best source for a healthy, stable puppy is a conscientious Husky breeder (sometimes called a hobby breeder). Finding a breeder you can trust and who has experience with the breed may take

Selecting the right breeder is the first step in finding the pup for you. An excellent reputation, strict breeding ethics and friendly personality are qualities you should look for.

time, but a good pup is worth the extra effort. Don't bother reading this chapter if you're going to run out and buy the first Husky puppy you meet. Too often this happens, and the guilty indulgent buyers are likely well-educated, sensible people who are rendered "ga-ga" by a blue-eyed baby dog. For your own sake—your money and your heart—slow down and make a smart choice.

There is nothing more seductive than a pair of perfectly bred Siberian puppies. Make sure the breeder meets your qualifications before committing to a puppy.

A breeder-puppy search can be an emotionally trying experience, taxing your patience and your willpower. All puppies are adorable and it's easy to fall in love with the first cute pup you see. But a poorly bred Husky will have health and temperament problems that can empty your wallet and break your heart. So do your breeder homework before you visit those cute pups. Arm yourself with a list of questions for the breeder (a good one won't object). Then leave your wallet and your kids at home

Try not to fall in love with the first Siberian baby your meet.

so you aren't tempted to take home a poorly bred but nonetheless irresistible Husky pup.

For starters, ask to see the pedigree and American Kennel Club (AKC) registration papers. The pedigree should include three to five generations of ancestry. Inquire about any titles in the pedigree, such as "Ch.", "CD" or "MA." Titles indicate a dog's accomplishments in some area of canine competition, which proves the merits of the ancestors and adds to the breeder's credibility. Titles can be for conformation showing, obedience and agility. You may also see health clearances for hips and eyes. While it is true that a pedigree and registration papers do not guarantee health or good temperament, a well-constructed pedigree is still a good insurance policy.

Ask why the breeder planned this litter. A conscientious breeder plans a litter of Huskies for specific reasons and should explain the genetics behind this particular breeding and what he expects the breeding to produce. He never breeds because "his Husky is sweet and/or beautiful, his neighbor's dog is handsome, they will have lovely puppies, his kids needed to experience puppy birth" and so on. Just loving his dog like crazy does not qualify an individual to breed dogs intelligently or properly raise a litter of Husky pups.

HEALTH COMES FIRST
Ask about health issues. Siberians are one of the few breeds least affected by hip dysplasia, thanks to the ongoing efforts of dedicated Husky breeders. The only way to produce puppies that are not affected by hip dysplasia and other genetic diseases is to screen the parents for those defects.

Many breeders also screen close relatives to build a pedigree with healthy hip depth. Ask the breeder if the sire and dam have hip clearances from OFA (Orthopedic

The Husky's eyes are not as healthy as his hips. Huskies are most prone to hereditary or juvenile cataracts, corneal dystrophy and progressive retinal

Visiting the breeder allows you to see the mother and the entire litter, all of whom should appear alert, sound and healthy, and happy to meet you.

Foundation for Animals, a national canine hip registry). These may be notated in the pedigree such as "OFA 'Good.'"

atrophy (PRA). All breeding stock should be examined annually and should be cleared during the year prior to breeding.

Damage from a cataract can range from a mild decrease in eyesight to complete blindness in extreme cases. Corneal dystrophy causes an abnormal collection of lipids in the cornea, resulting in a hazy opacity in the eye. The PRA that affects the Husky is unique to the breed and found only in Siberians and humans. It will cause a loss of day vision, and eventually total blindness. Affected males can go completely blind at five months of age.

Eye problems can occur in any eye color. Breeders should have the sire and dam examined by a specialist who is board-certified by the American College of Veterinary Ophthalmology (ACVO) and register the test results with the Canine Eye Registration Foundation (CERF). The Siberian Husky Club of America (SHCA) also has its own eye registry called the Siberian Husky Ophthalmologic Registry, which accepts ACVO exams and issues a certificate that is valid for one year. Good breeders will gladly, in fact, proudly, provide such documents.

An informed owner is the best owner of all. For more information on genetic disease in Siberian Huskies, you can contact the SHCA by email at www.shca.org/shcahp2a.html.

ASSESSING A BREEDER
Experienced Husky breeders are frequently involved in some aspect of the dog fancy with their dog(s), perhaps showing or training them for some type of performance event or dog-related activity. Their Husky(s) may have earned titles in various competitions, which is added proof of the breeder's experience and commitment to the breed. Dedicated breeders also may belong to the SHCA, a regional breed club or an area all-breed club.

Such affiliation with other experienced breeders and sportsmen expands their knowledge of their chosen breed, which further enhances their credibility. If the breeder is not "interested in showing," move along! No champions in a line means that the breeder alone thinks his dogs are good enough to breed. Finding puppies from champion lines means that at least three experienced show judges publicly agree with the breeder's assertion that his dogs are worth breeding!

Responsible breeders, by the way, do not raise several different breeds of dogs or produce multiple litters of pups throughout the year; one or two litters a year is typical of a hobby breeder. Some larger kennels have the staff and reputation to produce five or six litters a year, but these are quite exceptional.

The breeder will ask you questions, too... about your experience with dogs, your knowledge of Huskies, your previous dogs, etc. He also will want to know about your living arrangements, including your house, yard,

Good breeders spend time handling and socializing each pup in the litter to ease the pups' transition from the litter to their new human "packs."

kids, etc.; your goals for this pup and how you plan to raise it. His primary concern is the future of the puppies and whether you and your family will be suitable owners who will provide a safe and loving home for his precious little one. You should be suspicious of any breeder who agrees to sell you a Husky puppy without any type of interrogation process. Such indifference indicates a lack of concern about the pups, and casts doubt on the breeder's ethics and breeding program.

A good breeder also will warn you about the downside of the Husky. No breed of dog is perfect, nor is every breed suitable for every person's temperament and lifestyle. The Husky is a most unique breed of dog. Be prepared to weigh the bad news with the good about the Husky.

Most reputable breeders have a puppy sales contract that includes specific health guarantees and reasonable return policies. They should be willing to accept a puppy back if it does not work out. They also should be willing, indeed anxious, to check up

on the puppy's progress after he leaves home, and be available if you have questions or problems with the pup.

Many breeders place their pet-quality puppies on the AKC Limited Registration. This does register the pup with AKC and allows the owner to compete in AKC obedience competition, but does not allow AKC registration of any offspring from the mature dog. The purpose of Limited Registration is to prevent indiscriminate breeding of "pet-quality" dogs. The breeder, and only the breeder, can cancel the Limited Registration if the adult dog develops into breeding quality.

If you have any doubts at all, feel free to ask for references…and check with them. It's unlikely that a breeder will offer names of unhappy puppy clients, but calling other owners may make you more comfortable dealing with a particular breeder.

You can expect to pay a dear price for all of these breeder qualities, whether you purchase a "pet-quality" Husky for a companion dog or one for show or working potential. The bargain Husky in vet expenses and heartache that can't be measured in dollars and cents.

FINDING A BREEDER

So how do you find a reputable breeder whom you

When meeting the litter, one puppy may knock your snowshoes off. Follow your heart and the breeder's advice.

is not a bargain at all. Indeed, the discount pup is in reality a potential disaster that has a limited chance of developing into a healthy, stable adult. Such "bargains" could ultimately cost you a fortune can trust? Do your homework before you visit puppies. Ask your veterinarian, and if you don't have one, ask a friend's vet for a referral. Spend a day at a dog show or another dog event where you can meet

A pretty portrait of a proud mom and her beautiful puppy.

breeders and exhibitors and get to know their dogs. Most Husky devotees are more than happy to show off their dogs and brag about their accomplishments. If you know a Husky you are fond of, ask the owner where they got their dog.

Check with the American Kennel Club for breeder referrals in your area. Its website (www.akc.org) also offers links to Siberian Husky breed clubs and breeders throughout the United States. Breeder listings from the SHCA can also be found on the Siberian Husky website: www.shca.org/shcahp2a.html. Any bit of information you can glean will make you a smarter shopper when you visit a litter of pups.

When it's time to look for your Siberian Husky puppy, skip the newspaper ads. Reputable breeders rarely advertise in newspapers— they don't have to. They are very particular about prospective puppy owners and do not rely on mass advertising to attract the right people. Rather they depend on referrals from other breeders and previous puppy clients. And they are more than willing to keep any puppy past the usual seven- or eight-week placement age until the right person comes along.

Buying a puppy is not an impulse buy. You are not buying new boots or some luxury item on sale at the local mall. Fortunately, most pet shops don't sell puppies these days, but you also want to avoid "backyard breeders." These are small for-profit operations that are concerned only with bottom-line profit, not the health and well-being of the puppies they mass-produce. Even if you "just want a nice pet," you still want a *healthy* pup with a *sound* disposition. A good breeder is your best and only choice.

Perhaps the second most important ingredient in your breeder search is patience. You will not likely find the right breeder or litter on your first go-around. Good breeders often have waiting lists, but a good pup is worth the wait.

SELECTING A HUSKY BREEDER

Overview

- To locate a responsible, knowledgeable breeder, contact the American Kennel Club or the Siberian Husky Club of America.
- Visit a dog show to meet breeders and handlers of well-bred dogs.
- Begin your search patiently and with the right information. Have a list of questions ready for the breeder.
- When you're talking to the breeder, inquire about pedigrees, sales agreements, health clearances, registration papers and references.
- A reputable breeder will offer you information about any hereditary diseases in his line and any known problems he's encountered.

Finding the Right Puppy

Selecting the right puppy is paramount to a successful life with a Siberian Husky. You have to be prepared to spend time with the breeder, the puppies and their dam before you make your final choice. If possible, visit several litters and keep notes on what you see and like... and *don't* like...about each one. You may have to travel to visit a good litter, but your research, time, miles and dollars will pay off.

A puppy visit involves much more than puppy hugs and kisses. It's more like your ultimate job interview.

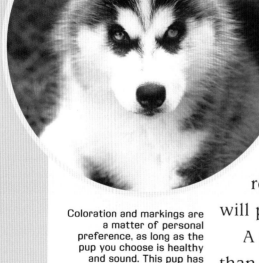

Coloration and markings are a matter of personal preference, as long as the pup you choose is healthy and sound. This pup has attractive dark markings and intense blue eyes, quite a striking combination.

While searching for your new Husky family member, you'll be checking out the applicants… the puppies and their parents, the breeder, as well as the living environment in which the pups are raised.

The more outgoing pups will be excited about your visit and come running, eager to introduce themselves.

Where and how a litter of pups is raised is vitally important to their early development into confident and social pets. The litter should be kept indoors, in the house or in an adjoining sheltered area, not isolated in a basement, garage or outside kennel. Husky puppies need to be socialized daily with people and people activities. The greater their exposure to household sights and sounds between four and seven weeks of age, the easier their adjustment to life with their future human family.

During your visit, scrutinize the puppies as well as their environment for cleanliness and signs of sickness or poor health. The pups and their

What a sweet face! This Siberian Husky puppy has the breed's characteristic odd eyes, one blue and one brown.

living area should be reasonably clean, (allowing for normal non-stop "puppy-pies"). The pups should appear energetic, bright-eyed and alert. Healthy pups have clean, thick coats, are well proportioned and feel solid and muscular without being overly fat and pot-bellied. Watch for crusted eyes or nose and any watery discharge from the nose, eyes or ears. Check for evidence of watery or bloody stools.

Visit with the dam and the sire if possible. Frequently the sire is not on premises, but the breeder should have photos and a résumé of his characteristics and accomplishments.

Pay special attention to the personality of the parents. Huskies are friendly but, like all Nordic or Spitz dogs, can be somewhat aloof with strangers, and should not shy away from a friendly overture. It is also normal for the dam to be somewhat protective of her young, but overly aggressive behavior is unacceptable. Temperament is inherited, and if one or both parents are very shy or insecure, it is likely that some of the pups will inherit those characteristics.

Observe the interactions of the dam with her pups, and notice how the pups react to their littermates and their surroundings, especially their response to people. They should be active and outgoing. In most Husky litters, some pups will be more outgoing than others, but even a quiet pup that is properly socialized should not be shy or spooky or shrink from a friendly voice or outstretched hand.

The breeder should be honest in discussing any differences in puppy personalities. Although many breeders do some type of temperament testing, they also have spent most of the past seven or eight weeks cuddling and cleaning up after these pups, and by now know the subtle differences in each pup's personality. The breeder's observations are valuable aids in selecting a Husky puppy that will be compatible with you and your lifestyle.

Tell the breeder if you plan to show your pup in confor-mation or compete in obedience and agility events or sled-dog activities. Some pups will show more promise than others, and the breeder can help you select one that will best suit your long-term goals.

Do you prefer a male or female? Which one is right for you? Both sexes are loving and loyal, and the differences are due to individual person-alities rather than gender. The Husky female is a gentle soul who is easy to live with. She also can be a bit more moody, depending on her whims and hormonal peaks. The male, who can be equally loyal and

very closely bonding to his master, is often up to 2 inches taller than the female and overall bigger and more powerful. Although males tend to be more even tempered than bitches, they are also more physical and

Once at your home, it may take a little while for the Husky pup to feel comfortable. It's an overwhelming experience, so give him time to come out of his shell.

exuberant during adoles-cence, which can be problematic in a strong and powerful dog. An untrained male also can become dominant with people and other dogs. A solid foundation in obedience is necessary if you want the dog to respect you as his leader. Intact males tend to be more territorial, especially with other male dogs.

In male puppies, both testicles should be descended into the scrotum. A dog with undescended testicles will make a fine pet, but will be ineligible to compete in the show ring.

Spaying or neutering your Siberian Husky if you don't aspire to show or breed creates a level playing field and eliminates most of those gender differences. He or she may live longer, too. What better reason to spay and neuter your Siberian Husky?

By seven weeks of age, the pups should have had at least one worming, a first puppy shot, and a vet certificate verifying he is in good health at the time of the exam. Some Husky breeders feel that separating the vaccines in a puppy's booster shots reduces the possibility of negative reactions to the various components in the combination vaccines. Ask your breeder and your veterinarian for their recommendations

The breeder should tell you what the pups have been eating, when and how much. Some send home a small supply of puppy food for the first few days. Most breeders also give their clients a puppy "take-home" packet that includes a copy of the health

Roughhousing and play-fighting among littermates are a part of early socialization and learning the rules of the pack.

certificate, the puppy's pedigree and registration papers, copies of the parents' health clearances and the breeder's sales contract if he has one. Many supply literature on the breed and how to properly raise a Siberian Husky pup. Dedicated breeders know that...the more you know...the better life will be for their precious Husky pups. Perhaps you

Your chosen pup should be physically sound and have a sturdy little body.

were lucky enough to select a breeder who cared enough to give you this book!

FINDING THE RIGHT PUPPY

Overview

- Don't buy a puppy from a catalog, a mall window or a cardboard box on the street corner. This is one of the most important purchases of your life.
- You are searching for a healthy, sound puppy. Don't be seduced by those shiny blue eyes and fuzzy coat (though clear eyes and soft, shiny coats are definite plusses).
- Inspect the environment of the kennel to make sure it's clean and good smelling. Ask to meet the dam (and sire) of the litter. Observe the interaction of the dam with her litter.
- Discuss your preference of a male or female with the breeder. He can tell you more about differences in his line.
- Owners who intend to show their Husky puppies should defer to the breeder's opinion about which pup is best suited for showing. Trust the breeder's insight in his line. That's part of what you're paying for.

Welcoming the Husky

Puppy-proofing is more than just a cute phrase in puppy training books. It is an essential part of your new Husky puppy's homecoming. A thorough puppy-proofing will prevent any accidents or surprises that could be dangerous and even fatal for your pup, and should be done before you bring your puppy home. Stock up on puppy essentials before your pup comes home. You won't have time after he arrives. Puppy shopping is great fun, but hang on to your purse strings. Puppy

Most importantly, welcome your Husky puppy home with lots of love!

stuff, especially the non-essentials, is often too cute to resist, so "stocking up" can easily decimate your budget. Start with basic essentials, and save the puppy goodies until later.

Not exactly what food bowls are intended for, but more fun for the puppies!

FOOD AND WATER BOWLS

You'll need two separate serving pieces, one for food and one for water. Stainless steel pans are your best choices as they are chew-proof and easy to clean. Huskies have strong jaws and love to chew. Some have been know to chew up their aluminum bowls. Plastic is much too flimsy, and those cute ceramic bowls break easily. Tip-proof is a good idea, since most puppies love to splash about in their water bowls, and the Husky is no exception.

Your yard and any areas to which your Husky pup has access must be puppy-proofed for the inquisitive explorer.

PUPPY FOOD

No matter what age your Siberian Husky is, he requires a high-quality food based on animal protein. Since the breed was developed by an Arctic peoples with a hunting/fishing economy in a region where plant life is non-existent, the Husky digests animal protein more efficiently than plant matter. Many puppy foods contain

Three types of collars (clockwise from top left): buckle collar, harness and choke.

soy products and these should be avoided for the Husky.

Siberian Huskies are efficient in digesting their food and require a smaller amount of food for their size than other dogs. A food formulated to meet the high-energy demands of active, hard-working adults proves satisfactory for all stages of the Husky's life. Select a meat- or fish-based food with a 26 to 34% protein content and a 18 to 20% fat content.

COLLARS AND ID TAGS

Your Husky pup should have an adjustable collar that will expand to fit him as he grows. Lightweight nylon adjustable collars work best for both pups and adult dogs. To fit properly, you should be able to slip two fingers between the collar and your puppy's neck. The ID tag should have your phone number, name and address, but not the puppy's name; as that would enable a stranger to identify and call your dog. Some owners include a line that says "Dog needs medication," to hopefully speed the dog's return if he is lost or stolen. Put the collar on as soon as the pup comes home so he can get used to wearing it. It's best to use an "O" ring for the tag, as the "S" ring snags on carpets and comes off easily.

Today even dog collars have gone high tech. Some come equipped with beepers and tracking devices. The most advanced pet identification tool uses a Global Positioning System and fits inside a collar or tag. When your dog leaves its programmed home perimeter, the device sends a message directly to your phone or email address.

Choke collars are for training purposes and should be worn only during training sessions. Training collars should never be used on Husky puppies under 16 weeks of age.

LEASHES

For your own convenience and for puppy's safety, his leash closet should include at least two kinds of leads. A narrow 6-foot leather leash is best for walks, puppy kindergarten and obedience class and leash-training workouts. The other lead you should buy is a flexible lead. Flexible leads are extendable leads housed in a large handle. They extend and retract with the push of a button. This is the ideal tool for exercising and should be a staple in

A collar and ID tag are parts of a well-dressed Husky's everyday wardrobe.

every puppy's wardrobe. Flexible leads are available in several lengths (8 feet to 26 feet) and strengths, depending on breed size. Longer is better, as it allows your dog to run about and check out the good sniffing areas farther from you. Flexible leads are especially handy for exercising your puppy in unfenced areas or when traveling with your dog.

BEDDING

Dog beds are just plain fun. Beds run the gamut from small and inexpensive to elegant, high-end beds suitable for the most royal of dog breeds. However, don't go overboard just yet. Better to save that fancy bed for when your Husky is older and less apt to shred it up or make a mess on it. For puppy bedding, it's best to use a large towel, mat or blanket that can be easily laundered (which will probably be often).

CRATING AND GATING

These will be your most important puppy purchases. A crate is your most valuable tool for housebreaking your pup and his most favorite place to feel secure. Crates come in three varieties, wire mesh, fabric mesh and the more familiar plastic, airline-type crate. Wire or mesh-fabric crates offer the best ventilation and some conveniently fold up suitcase-style, although a mesh crate might be a little risky for a youngster who likes to dig and chew. Whatever your choice, purchase an adult-size crate, about 20 inches wide

Choose a crate for your puppy that will house him as an adult, too. The crate will become his den for life.

by 30 inches long, rather than one that is small or puppy size; your Husky will soon grow into it. Crates are available at most pet stores and through pet-supply catalogs.

A well-placed baby gate will protect your house from the inevitable puppy mischief, and thus save your sanity as well. It's wise to confine puppy to a tiled or uncarpeted room or space, one that is accessible to the outside door he will use for potty trips. Gated to a safe area where he cannot wreak havoc or destruction, the puppy will soon master Housebreaking 101, learn to chew only appropriate toys rather than your antique furniture, and save himself from unnecessary corrections for normal puppy mishaps.

Gated, however, does not mean unsupervised. Siberian Husky puppies will chew out of boredom and can destroy the indestructible. If the

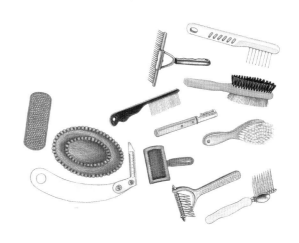

puppy must be unattended, use his crate.

GROOMING TOOLS

Huskies are naturally clean dogs that have no unpleasant body odor. Their dense coat requires frequent brushing to keep it well groomed and mat-free. The Husky sheds his coat at least once a year, which can be a problem for fastidious housekeepers. A slicker brush and mat rake are good starter grooming tools. Be sure to ask your breeder for advice on proper grooming tools.

Introduce your puppy to

A gamut of grooming supplies are available at your pet shop. Choose wisely and buy the best you can afford.

CHAPTER 6

grooming early on so he learns to like it. It also helps to condition the pup to hands-on attention, which will be invaluable when you have to clean his teeth and ears and clip his nails.

Check your yard and landscaping for any plants that may be dangerous to dogs, and either get rid of them or prevent your Husky from gaining access to those areas.

HOUSEHOLD HAZARDS

After puppy shopping, you must puppy-proof your house. Husky pups are naturally curious critters that will investigate everything new, then seek-and-destroy just because it's fun. The message here is…Never let your puppy roam your house unsupervised.

Trash cans and diaper pails are natural puppy magnets. Keep these closed and out of puppy's reach. Puppies don't outgrow their love of stinky stuff, so this will be one of your house rules. Lock up medication bottles, cleaning materials and roach and rodent poisons. You'll be amazed at what a determined puppy can find.

Unplug electrical cords wherever you can and make the others inaccessible. Injuries from chewed electrical cords are extremely common in young dogs.

Siberian Husky puppies snuffling about at ground level will find and ingest the tiniest of objects and will end up in surgery. Keep dental floss, yarn, needles and thread, and other stringy stuff away from the pup. If you have toilet-bowl cleaners, throw them out now. All dogs are born with toilet sonar and quickly discover that the water there is always cold.

In the house, pick up after yourself including socks and underwear, shoes and slippers, too. The author but your socks and undies smell like "mommy times ten!" and what could be more appealing to an olfactory-fixated canine? Most vets will

Whether in a kennel run or a yard, secure fencing of adequate height is necessary for safely containing the athletic Husky.

doesn't mean to sound like your nagging mother or wife! In truth, puppies love all of these good-smelling objects. Keep them off the floor and close your closet doors. It may not be obvious to you, reluctantly tell you stories about the stuff they surgically removed from a puppy's gut.

In your garage, beware of antifreeze! It is extremely toxic and even a few drops will kill an adult Husky, less for a pup. Also, keep fertilizers away from your nosy Husky's sniffer. Lock these up well out of reach.

That's it for inanimate objects, but how about other four-foot creatures in your home? Huskies have strong predatory instincts and view many small animals as prey. Guinea pigs, hamsters, rabbits, mice and cats are at risk in and around the home. You cannot change this natural behavior. Likewise, your family parrot or cockatoo is at danger, too, even though he only has two feet! Winged pets must be carefully monitored with a Husky, who may or may not accept "a wild falcon" flying around his crate.

SOCIALIZATION

This actually puppy-proofs your puppy, not your house. Puppy socialization is your Husky's insurance policy to a happy, stable adulthood, and is, without question, the most important element in a Husky puppy's introduction to the human world. Huskies are by nature gregarious with people and other dogs and are rarely aggressive or suspicious of strangers. However, it has been proven that unsocialized pups grow up to be spooky and insecure, and fearful of people, children and strange places. Many turn into fear biters or become aggressive with other dogs, strangers, even family members. Such dogs can seldom be rehabilitated and often end up abandoned in animal shelters where they are ultimately euthanized. Puppy socialization lays the foundation for a well-behaved, adult canine, thus preventing those canine behaviors that lead to abandonment and euthanasia.

The primary socialization period occurs during the puppy's first 20 weeks of life. Once he leaves the safety of his mom and littermates at seven to ten weeks of age, your job begins. Start with a quiet, uncomplicated household for the first day or two, then gradually introduce him to the sights and sounds of his new human world. Frequent interaction with

situations upbeat and positive, which will create a positive attitude toward future encounters.

"Positive" is especially important when visiting your veterinarian. You don't want a

A chew toy is a good way to focus the pup's energies in a positive manner, as well as saving your belongings from the damage that a bored puppy can inflict.

children, new people and other dogs are essential at this age. Visit new places (dog-friendly, of course) like parks or even the local grocery store parking lot where there are crowds of people. Set a goal of two new places a week for the next two months. Keep these new

pup that quakes with fear every time he sets a paw inside his doctor's office. Make sure your vet is a dog lover as well as a dog doctor.

Your puppy also will need supervised exposure to children. Huskies are generally good with young-sters, but both dog and child must learn how to behave properly with each other. Puppies of all breeds tend to view little people as litter-mates and will try to exert the upper paw (a dominance ploy) over the child. Children must be taught how to properly play with the dog and to respect his privacy. Likewise, adult family members should supervise and teach the puppy not to nip or jump up on the kids.

Take your Husky youngster to puppy school. Some classes accept pups from 10 to 12 weeks of age, with one series of puppy shots as a health requirement. The younger the pup, the easier it is to shape good behavior patterns. A good puppy class teaches proper canine social etiquette rather than rigid obedience skills. Your puppy will meet and play with young dogs of other breeds, and you will learn about the positive teaching tools you'll need to train your pup. Puppy class is important for both novice and experienced puppy folks.

Having some treats on hand will help your puppy feel right at home in no time.

If you're a smart Husky owner, you won't stop there and will continue on with a basic obedience class. Of course you want the best behaved Husky in the neighborhood.

Remember this: there is a direct correlation between the quality and amount of time you spend with your puppy during his first 20 weeks of life and the character of the adult dog he will become. You cannot recapture this valuable learning period, so make the most of it.

The day that your Husky puppy comes home marks the start of a wonderful friendship with one of the best canine companions around.

WELCOMING THE HUSKY

Overview

- Time to go shopping! Your pet store is waiting for you, and the attendants will be more than happy to help you on your puppy shopping spree.
- On your list are: puppy food, bowls, a collar and a ID tag, a leash and collar, a crate, a gate, grooming tools, and one or two safe chew toys.
- Before the puppy prances across the threshold, make sure that your house and yard have been Husky-proofed.
- Even though Huskies love people and other dogs, socialization is a vital part of his growing up. Make socialization experiences happy ones.
- Enroll your puppy in school. Obedience classes are an excellent way to socialize and train your new pup.

Husky Puppy Kindergarten

A treat is a surefire way to get your Husky's attention, as well as a welcome reward for a job well done.

Puppy class and follow-up obedience training are especially important for the Siberian Husky. The trainability quotient for the breed is moderately low as Huskies can be resistant to obedience training. However, if you want to live in harmony with your Husky, you have to be the "top dog" in his life, and obedience training is the only way to accomplish that. Puppy kindergarten starts the day you bring your puppy home.

All dogs are pack animals, and as such, they need a leader. Your Husky's first boss was his dam, and all of his life lessons came from his mom and littermates. When he played too rough or nipped too hard, his siblings cried and the game stopped. When he got pushy or obnoxious, his dam cuffed him gently with a maternal paw. Now you have to assume the role of dam and leader and communicate appropriate behavior in terms his little canine mind will understand. Remember, too, that from a canine point of view, human rules make no sense at all.

You want your Husky to look up to you always, not just because there's a treat in your hand!

When you start the teaching process, keep this thought uppermost: The first 20 weeks of any canine's life is his most valuable learning time, a period when his mind is best able to soak up every lesson, both positive and negative. Positive experiences and proper socialization during this period are critical to his future development and stability. Keep this golden rule of socialization in mind: the amount and

Young puppies naturally "follow the leader," but Huskies soon become more independent, with minds of their own. Puppy training must start young, especially with a breed like the Husky.

quality of time you invest with your Husky youngster now will determine what kind of an adult he will become. Wild dog or a gentleman or lady? Well-behaved or naughty dog? It's up to you.

Canine behavioral science tells us that any behavior that is rewarded will be repeated

Positive reinforcement is the way to go in your training endeavors. Your dog will savor a pat and your praise as much as any food reward.

(called positive reinforcement). If something good happens, like a tasty treat or a scratch on the head, the puppy will naturally want to repeat the behavior. That same research also has proven that the best way to a puppy's mind is through his stomach. A similar rule applies to human husbands. Never underestimate the power of a cookie (or steak)! This leads to a very important puppy rule: keep your pockets loaded with puppy treats at all times, so you are prepared to reinforce good behavior whenever it occurs.

That same reinforcement principle also applies to negative behavior or what we humans (not the dog) might consider negative (like rooting through the trash can, which the dog thinks is good smelly fun and not "wrong"). If the pup gets into the garbage, steals food or does anything else that makes him feel good, he will do it again. What better reason to keep a sharp eye on your puppy?

You are about to begin Puppy Class 101. Rule Number

One: The puppy must learn that you are now the "alpha" dog and his new pack leader. Rule Number Two: You have to teach him in a manner he will understand (sorry, barking just won't do it.). Remember always that he knows nothing about human standards of behavior.

WORD ASSOCIATION

Use the same word (command) for each behavior every time you teach it, adding food rewards and verbal praise to reinforce the positive. The pup will make the connection and will be motivated to repeat the behavior when he hears those key words. For example, when teaching the pup to potty outside, use the same potty term ("Go potty," "Get busy" or "Hurry up" are commonly used) each time he eliminates, adding a "Good boy!" while he's urinating. The pup will soon learn what those trips outside are for.

TIMING

All dogs learn their lessons in the present tense. You have to catch them in the act (good or bad) in order to dispense rewards or discipline. You have three to five seconds to connect with him or he will not understand what he did wrong. Thus timing and consistency are your keys to success in teaching any new behavior or correcting bad behaviors.

Successful puppy training depends on several important principles.

1. Use simple one-word commands and say them only once. Otherwise the puppy learns that "Come" (or "Sit" or "Down") is a two- or three-word command (like the "Do Run Run").

2. Never correct your dog for something he did minutes earlier. Three to five seconds, remember?

3. Always praise (and offer a treat) as soon as he does

something good (or stops doing something naughty). How else will the puppy know he's a good dog?

4. Be consistent. You can't snuggle together on the couch to watch TV today, then scold him for climbing on the couch tomorrow.

5. Never tell your dog to come, then correct him for something he did wrong. He will think the correction is for coming to you. (Think like a dog, remember?) Always go to the dog to stop unwanted behavior, but be sure to catch him *in the act* or your correction will not be understood.

6. Never hit or kick your dog or strike him with a newspaper or other object. Such physical measures will only create fear and confusion in your dog and could provoke aggressive behavior down the road.

7. When praising or

correcting, use your best doggie voice. Use a light and happy voice for praise, and a firm, sharp voice for warnings or corrections. A whiny "No, No" or "Drop that" will not sound convincing, nor will a deep, gruff voice make your puppy feel like he's been a good fellow. Likewise, use your own voice when talking to your dog—don't "baby-talk."

Your dog also will respond accordingly to family arguments. If there's a shouting match, he will think that he did something wrong and head for cover. So never argue in front of the kids...or the dog!

Despite the Husky's powerful appearance, he is a soft dog who will not respond to harsh training methods or corrections. Puppy kindergarten and continued lessons in obedience are the best course to combating the Husky's stubborn streak.

You must teach your puppy always to come when you call him. Trainers have been successful teaching the "come" by approaching it as a game.

PUPPY GAMES

Puppy games are a great way to entertain your puppy and yourself, while subliminally teaching lessons in the course of having fun. Start with a game plan and a pocketful of tasty dog treats. Keep your games short so you don't push his attention span beyond Husky-puppy limits. Huskies get bored with too much repetition.

Puppy Catch-Me—This one helps teach the come command. With two people sitting on the floor about 10 or 15 feet apart, one person holds and pets the pup while the other calls him, "Puppy, puppy, come!" in a happy voice. When the pup comes running, lavish him with big hugs and give a tasty treat. Repeat back and forth several times...don't over do it.

You can add a ball or toy and toss it back and forth for the puppy to retrieve. When he picks it up, praise and hug some more, give him a goodie to release the toy, then toss the ball back to person number two. Repeat as above.

Hide and Seek—Another game that teaches "Come." Play this game outdoors in your yard or other confined

Crates have many uses. This crate is fine for the pup's travel crate (for now), but he will outgrow it in no time. It's best to have the Husky's adult size in mind when purchasing a crate for use in the home.

safe area. When the pup is distracted, hide behind a tree. Peek out to see when he discovers that you are gone and comes running back to find you (trust me, he will do that). As soon as he gets close, come out, squat down with arms outstretched and call him, "Puppy, come!" This is also an excellent bonding aid and teaches the puppy to depend on you.

Where's Your Toy?—Start by placing one of his favorite toys in plain sight and ask your puppy, "Where's your toy?" and let him take it. Then place your puppy safely outside the room and place the toy where only part of it shows. Bring him back and ask the same question. Praise highly when he finds it. Repeat several times. Finally, conceal the toy completely and let your puppy sniff it out. Trust his nose…he will find his toy.

Husky puppies love to have fun with their people. Games are excellent teaching aids, and one of the best ways to say "I love you" to your Husky.

HUSKY PUPPY KINDERGARTEN

Overview

- "Mush" may be the only command that your Husky really understands. Running is fun and easy. The rest of obedience class doesn't really interest the Husky.
- Start teaching your Husky puppy as early as possible, emphasize positive training and give him lots of love and liver.
- Two important rules: be the "lead dog" (the "alpha") and know how to communicate with your dog.
- Teach word association for basic behaviors.
- It's all in the timing: Learn the seven rules to successful puppy training.
- Play the three games with your puppy to teach him to come to you.

House-training Your Husky

If you think a dog crate or confinement is cruel and unusual punishment, you might rethink your decision about living with a Siberian Husky. The Husky is a working sled dog and, true to his heritage, he loves to run. It is the single most distinctive quality that sets the Nordic dogs apart from other dogs. He will bolt at the first opportunity, and a dash across a busy street can cost him his life. Thus, a crate, a fence, a kennel, each promise a safe life for your Husky.

Further, if you understand the canine mind, you know that canines are natural den creatures, due to the

Training your dog to relieve himself outdoors is essential to clean living and a happy relationship with your dog.

thousands of years their ancestors spent living in caves and earthen dens. Most pups adapt naturally to crate confinement, and Husky pups, more primitive than many of the more "refined" (or "unnatural") breeds, adjust in no time.

Follow your nose! The pup's keen sense of smell will lead him to his relief site, and soon he will know where to "go" with no problem.

Puppies also are inherently clean and hate to soil their "den" or living space, which makes the crate a natural house-training aid. Thus, the crate is actually a multi-purpose dog accessory: your Husky's personal dog house within your house; a humane house-training tool; a security measure that will keep the puppy out of household dangers and protect your home and antique furniture when you're not home; a travel aid to house and protect your dog when traveling (most motels will accept a crated dog); and, finally, a comfy dog space for your puppy when delivery or service people or your anti-dog relatives come to visit.

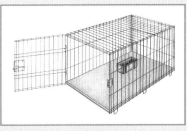

The wire crate is the best choice for Husky owners. Ventilation, easy clean-up and a good view are solid advantages.

Many experienced breeders insist on crate use after their puppy leaves, and some begin crate-training their pups before they send the pups home. Nevertheless, let's assume that your Husky has never seen a crate, so it's up to you to make sure his introduction is a pleasant one.

When first introducing your puppy to his crate, toss a tiny treat into the crate to entice him to go in and continue doing so for the first day or two. Pick a crate command, such as "Kennel," "Inside" or "Crate," and use it when he enters. Introduce the crate as soon as he comes home so he learns that this is his new "house." You also can feed his first few meals inside the crate with the door left open, so the crate association will be a happy one.

Make a practice of placing the puppy in his crate for naps, nighttime and whenever you are unable to watch him closely. Not to worry…he will let you know when he wakes up and needs a potty trip. If he falls asleep under the table and wakes up when you're not there, guess what he'll do first? Make a puddle, then toddle over to say "Hi!"

Become a Husky vigilante. Routines, consistency and an eagle eye are your keys to house-training success. Puppies always "go" when they wake up (quickly now!), after eating, after a play period and after time spent in their crate. Most pups under 12 weeks of age will need to eliminate at least every hour or so, or up to ten times a day. (Set your oven or microwave timer to remind you.)

Always take the puppy outside to the same area, telling him "Outside" as you go out. Pick a "potty" phrase, ("Hurry up," "Go potty" and "Get busy" are popular choices), and use it when he does his business, lavishing him with "Good puppy, get busy!" Always use the same exit door for these potty trips, and confine the puppy to the exit area so he can find it when he needs it. Watch for sniffing and circling, sure signs he needs to relieve himself. Don't allow him to roam the house until he's house-trained...how will he find that outside door if he's three or four rooms away? He does not have a house map in his head.

Of course, he will have accidents. All puppies do. If you catch him in the act, clap your hands loudly and say "Aaah! Aaah!" and scoop him up to go outside. Your voice should startle him and make him stop. (Well, maybe.) Be sure to praise when he finishes his duty outside.

If you discover the piddle spot after the fact...more than three or four seconds later...you're too late. Pups only understand in the

moment and will not understand a correction given more than five seconds (that's 1-2-3-4-5!) after the deed. Correcting any later will only cause fear and confusion. Just forget it and vow to be more vigilant.

Be patient and imagine how your puppy must be feeling with all your strange expectations and demands.

Control your frustration and be patient. Never ever rub your puppy's nose in his mistake or strike your puppy or adult dog with your hand, a newspaper or any other object to correct him. Would you strike an infant for wetting his diaper? Likewise, your puppy will not understand what he has done wrong and will only become fearful of the person who is hitting him. There is no place in dog training for hitting your dog.

Potty hint: Remove puppy's water after 7 p.m. at night to aid in nighttime bladder control. If he gets thirsty, offer him an ice cube. Then just watch him race for the refrigerator when he hears the rattle of the ice cube tray.

Despite its many benefits, the crate can be abused. Puppies under 12 weeks of age should never be confined for more than 2 hours at a time, unless, of course, they are sleeping. A general rule of thumb is three hours maximum for a three-month old pup, four or five hours for the four to five month old, and no more than six hours for dogs over six months of age. If you're unable to be home to release the dog, arrange for a relative, neighbor or dog-sitter to let him out to exercise and potty.

If you prefer to paper-train your Husky pup instead of crate-training him, the routine is basically the same (though not nearly as effective or tidy). Assign an out-of-the-way elimination place and cover it with newspaper. Take your puppy to the designated papered area on schedule. Use the specified potty word, and praise when he does his business. Do not use the area for any other purpose except potty breaks. Keep the area clean. You can place a small piece of soiled paper on the clean ones to remind puppy why he's there. His nose will tell him what to do.

What can you do with an uncrated puppy when you're not home? (Not a wise choice for a Husky puppy.) Confine him to one area with a dog-proof barrier (a baby gate will work for a while). Puppy-proofing the home in and of itself won't be enough as even in an empty room, a bored Husky pup may chew through drywall. An exercise pen 4 feet by 4 feet square (available through pet suppliers), sturdy enough that the pup can't knock it down, will provide safe containment for short periods. Paper one area for elimination, with perhaps an easily laundered blanket in the opposite corner for napping. Husky puppies are seldom content to lie around calmly

chomping on a chew toy. If you don't or won't crate and cannot supervise your pup, be prepared to pay the consequences (in dollars and aggravation).

Most importantly, remember that successful house-training revolves around consistency, repetition and word association. Maintain a strict schedule and use your key words consistently. Well-trained owners have well-trained pups, and clean houses!

HOUSE-TRAINING YOUR HUSKY

Overview

- Dogs are den creatures, and your dog's den is his crate.
- House-training means teaching the Husky clean indoor behavior, not as easy as it sounds for a dog who likes to live outside.
- Housebreaking requires the owner to become ever-watchful of his Husky's habits (eating, drinking, sleeping and relieving himself).
- Use a relief command so that your puppy will tell you when he needs to go outside.
- Monitor the puppy's water intake during housebreaking.
- Consider the crate-less approach by using newspaper and a dog gate.

Teaching Basic Commands

The Siberian Husky is born with "attitude." He is an independent creature with a low desire to do things your way. It is most prudent to start teaching your Husky puppy basic obedience commands before he matures and is more resistant to do your bidding. This is important if your Husky is to become a canine good citizen who will be welcome wherever he goes. He needs to learn those behaviors that will provide you with an element of control: come, sit, stay, down, wait and heel.

The Husky is born with the attitude for which he's notorious: this youngster's mischievous look says it all.

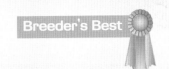

Always start your teaching exercises in a quiet, distraction-free environment. Once your pup has mastered any task, change the setting and practice in a different location... another room, outside in the yard, then with another person or a dog nearby. If the pup reacts to the new distraction and does not perform the exercise, back up your training, make his food rewards more enticing and continue with the exercise by working without distractions for a while.

It will take much dedication to progress to the level of show-ring training with your Husky.

Appoint one person to instruct your puppy in the early stages to not confuse the pup. It's the "too-many-cooks" rule of dog training. Once the puppy has learned a command reliably, other family members can join in. Ignore your Husky for a few minutes before a training session. The lack of stimulation will make him want your company and attention.

Take your Husky to distraction-free locations to practice the basic obedience commands. Always keep him on a leash when practicing in unfenced areas.

Keep sessions short, no longer than ten minutes at first, so your puppy won't get bored or lose his enthusiasm. In time he will be able to concentrate for longer periods. Watch for signs of boredom and loss of attention. Vary the exercises to keep his enthusiasm level high. Always keep your training sessions positive and upbeat. Use lots of praise, praise and more praise! Never train your dog or puppy if you are in a grumpy mood. You will lose patience and he will think it is his fault. That will reverse any progress the two of you have made.

Finish every training sessions on a positive note. If you have been struggling or unsuccessful, switch gears and do something he knows well (Sit) and end the session sitting happy.

Before you can effectively teach your puppy any command, two things must happen. The puppy must learn to respond to his name (name recognition), and you must be able to gain and hold his attention. How do you accomplish that? Why, with treats, of course! Treats are defined as tiny tidbits, preferably a soft easy-to-chew morsels. We don't want to over-feed this pup. Thin slices of hotdogs cut in quarters work non-kosher wonders.

ATTENTION AND NAME RECOGNITION

Start by calling puppy's name. Once. Not two or three times, but once. Otherwise your willful bitch will learn she has a three-part name ("Kala—Kala!—Kala Marie!!") and will ignore you when you say "Kala" once. Begin by using your dog's name when he is undistracted and you are sure that he will look at you and pop him a treat as soon as he does so. Repeat at least a dozen times, several times a day. It won't take more than a day or so before he understands that his name means something good to eat.

TAKE IT AND LEAVE IT

These two commands offer too many advantages to list. Place a treat in the palm of your hand and tell him "Take it" as he grabs the treat. Repeat three times. On the fourth time, do not say a word as your dog reaches for the treat…just close your fingers around the treat and wait. Do not pull away, but be prepared for pup to paw, lick, bark and nibble on your fingers. Patience! When he finally pulls away from your hand and waits a moment, open your hand and tell him "Take it."

A gentle push on the hindquarters will help the Husky into the proper sit position while he's learning.

Now the next step. Show your pup the treat in the palm of your hand and tell him to "Leave it." When he goes for the treat, close your hand, repeat "Leave it." Repeat this process until he pulls away and waits just a second. Then open your hand and tell him to "Take it." Repeat until he waits just a few seconds, then give the treat on "Take it." Gradually extend the time you wait before you tell him "Take it."

Now you want to teach your dog to leave things on the ground, not just your hand. (Think of all the things you don't want him to pick up.) Position yourself in front of your dog and toss a treat behind you and a little to the side so he can see it, while saying "Leave it." Here begins the dance. If he goes for the treat, use your body, not your hands, to block him, moving him backwards away from the treat. As soon as he backs off and gives up trying to get around you, unblock the treat and tell him "Take it." Be ready to block again if he goes for it before you give permission. Repeat the process until he understands and waits for the command.

Once he knows this well, practice with his food dish, telling him to "Leave it," then "Take it" after he complies (he can either sit or stand while waiting for his dish). As before, gradually extend the waiting period before you tell him "Take it."

This little training exercise sends many messages to your Husky. He is reminded that you're the boss and that all good things, like food, come from his almighty musher (his owner). Likewise, it will help prevent your puppy from becoming too possessive of his food bowl, a behavior that only escalates and leads to "resource guarding" and more serious aggressive behaviors.

COME COMMAND

Always practice this command on-leash. You can't afford to risk failure or the pup will learn he does not have to come when called. Once you have pup's attention, call him from a short distance, "Puppy, come!" (use your happy voice) and give a treat when he comes to you. Gently grasp and hold his collar with one hand as you dispense the treat. This is important. You will eventually phase out the treat and switch to hands-on praise. This maneuver also connects holding his collar with coming and getting a treat, which will assist you in countless future behaviors. Do 10 or 12 repetitions 2 or 3 times a day. Once the pup has mastered "come," continue to practice daily to burn this most important behavior in his tiny brain.

Because the Husky is genetically programmed to run, never practice with your dog off-leash or in an open area. In fact, on-leash is a lifetime practice when you own a Husky. One day he could hear that ancestral call of the wild and be off and running in a blink. Don't take that risk—tether his Nordic neck.

Daily obedience practice is another lifetime dog rule. Dogs will be dogs, especially Siberian Huskies, and if we don't maintain their skills, they will sink back into sloppy, inattentive behaviors that will be harder to correct. Incorporate these commands into your daily routine, and your Siberian Husky will

remain a gentleman you can be proud of.

SIT COMMAND

This one's a snap, since your puppy already understands the treat process. Stand in front of your pup, move the treat directly over his nose and slowly move it backwards. As he folds

In the sit/stay, the trainer uses verbal commands and a hand signal to convey to the dog that he is not to get up from the sit.

backwards to reach the goodie, his rear will move downward to the floor. If the puppy raises up to reach the treat, just lower it a bit. The moment his behind is down, tell him "Sit." That's one word: "Sit." Release the treat and gently grasp that collar as you did with the come. He will again make that positive connection between the treat, the sit, and the collar hold.

As time goes by, make him hold the sit position longer before you give the treat (the beginning of the stay

Practice using the sit command for everyday activities; do random sits throughout the day, always for a food or praise reward. Once he is reliable, combine the "Sit" and "Leave it" for his food dish. Your Husky is expanding his vocabulary.

DOWN COMMAND

With the puppy in the sit position, move the food lure from his nose to the ground and slightly backwards between his front paws. Wiggle it as necessary. As

The down command is never the easiest to teach. Extra reassurance, praise and, of course, treats, will help you accomplish this exercise.

command). Start using your release word ("Okay" or "At ease" will do fine) to release him from the sit position.

soon as his front legs and rear end hit the floor, give the treat and tell him "Down, good boy, down," thus connecting the word to the behavior. Down is a submissive posture and some dogs find it difficult to master. Be patient and be generous with the praise when he cooperates. Once he goes into the down position with ease, chain it to the stay command as you did with sit position. By six months of age, the puppy should be able to do a ten-minute solid sit-stay, ditto for a down-stay.

WAIT COMMAND

You'll love this one, especially when your fearless snow-plower comes in the house with wet or muddy paws after a morning of winter fun. Work on this with a closed door. Start to open the door as if to go through or out. When your dog tries to follow, step in front of him and body-block to prevent his passage through the door. Keep it up until he hesitates and you can open the door a little to pass through. Then say your release word and let him go

through. Repeat by body-blocking until he understands and waits for you, then start applying the wait command to the behavior. Practice in different doorways, using outside entrances (to safe or enclosed areas) after he will wait reliably.

HEEL COMMAND

The formal heel command comes a bit later in the learning curve. A young dog should be taught to walk calmly on a leash at or near your side. That is best accomplished when your pup is very young and small, instead of 30 or 40 pounds hauling you down the street.

Start leash training as soon as pup comes home. Simply attach it to his buckle collar and let him drag it around for a little while every day. Play a puppy game with the leash on. Make wearing his leash a happy moment in his day. If he chews the leash, distract him with a play activity. You can also spray the leash with a bitter deterrent to make it taste unpleasant.

After a few days, gather up the leash in a distraction-free zone…house or yard… and take just a few steps with your pup. With your puppy at your left side, hold a treat lure at his nose level to encourage him to walk next to you. Pat your knee and use a happy voice. Use the phrase "Let's go!" when you move forward, hold the treat to keep him near. Take a few steps, give the treat and praise. Move forward just a few steps each time.

Keep these sessions short and upbeat, a mere 30 seconds at a time. Never scold or nag him into walking faster or slower, just encourage him with happy talk. Walk straight

Daily walks will be a part of your everyday routine with your Husky. They will not be enjoyable for either of you unless the dog is trained to behave politely on lead.

ahead at first, adding wide turns once he gets the hang of it. Progress to 90-degree turns, using a gentle leash tug, a happy verbal "Let's go!" and, of course, a treat. Walk in short 30- to 40-second bursts, with a happy break (use your release word) and brief play (including some hugs) in between. Keep total training time short and always quit with success, even if just a few short steps.

Formal heeling will come much later with formal instruction in a basic obedience class. All of these behaviors are taught in some phase of a young dog training class. Check with your vet or a local kennel club to find one in your area. There are dozens of books written on positive methods of obedience training for puppies and adults. Buy one or more of these to get your dog's education off to a roaring start. You and your Husky will both be smarter for your efforts.

TEACHING BASIC COMMANDS

Overview

- The Husky is easily distracted, so start lessons in a place that is quiet and free from environmental distractions.
- Appoint one person to handle the Husky's training regimen.
- Begin by getting your puppy's attention.
- Be brief and concise. Huskies don't like repetition any more than you do.
- Finish every lesson on a positive note.
- Important first lessons include: name recognition, the release command, "Take it" and "Leave it."
- Here's your goal: teach the basic commands, including come, sit, stay, down, heel and wait.

Home Care for Your Husky

Your Husky should see his veterinarian at least once a year for health maintenance. Between those visits, you are in charge of your dog's health. The more you know about canine health issues, the better prepared you will be to raise a healthy, long-lived Siberian Husky.

Of all the regimens included in this chapter, two are, without question, the most important…weight control and dental hygiene. Veterinarians tell us that over 50% of the dogs they see are grossly overweight, and that such obesity will

Your Husky depends on you for good health and a good home. A dog who knows he's loved is a happy, healthy companion.

take two to three years off a dog's life, given the strain it puts on the animal's heart, lungs and joints. The obvious message here: lean is healthier.

WEIGHT CONTROL

To determine if your Husky is at a proper weight, you should be able to feel his ribs beneath a thin layer of muscle with very gentle pressure on his rib cage. When viewing your dog from above, you should be able to see a definite waistline, and from the side, he should have an obvious "tuck-up" in his abdomen.

Even the energetic Husky needs to rest, but if your dog seems lethargic or otherwise "not himself," a call to the vet is warranted.

Keep a record of his weight from each annual vet visit. A few extra pounds? Adjust his food portions (eliminate those table scraps), perhaps switch to a "light," "senior" or lower calorie dog-food formula, and increase his exercise.

Feel under the coat for anything carried in from the outdoors, as well as lumps, bumps, sores and the like.

Excessive weight is especially hard on older dogs with creaky joints.

Walking and running (slower for old guys) are still the best workouts for healthy maintenance. Tailor your Husky's exercise to fit his age and physical condition.

DENTAL CARE

The American Veterinary Dental Society states that, by age three, 80% of dogs exhibit signs of gum disease. Symptoms include yellow and brown build-up of tartar along the gumline, red and inflamed gums, and persistent bad breath. If neglected, these conditions will allow bacteria to enter your dog's bloodstream through those damaged gums, increasing the risk for disease in vital organs. These are common causes of death in older dogs...and highly preventable!

Your vet should examine your Husky's teeth and gums during his annual checkup. During the other 364 days a year, you are your Husky's dentist. Brush his teeth daily, or at least twice a week. Use a doggie toothbrush and use dog toothpaste flavored with chicken, beef or liver. (Minty people paste is harmful to dogs.) If he resists a brush, you can use a gauze pad or nappy cloth wrapped around your finger. You can also try a "finger-brush," which you can find at the pet shop. Start brushing with gentle gum massages when your Husky is very young.

Feeding dry dog food will help minimize plaque accumulation. You can also treat your dog to a raw carrot every day. Healthy chew objects, such as nylon or rubber bones and toys with ridges, act as tartar scrapers.

BODY CHECKS

Your weekly grooming sessions should include body checks for lumps, hot spots and other problems. A hot spot is an open sore caused by the dog's licking at his coat. Your vet should examine any abnormality. Black mole-like patches or growths on any body part require immediate veterinary inspection.

Be extra-conscious of dry skin, a flaky coat and thinning hair, all signs of possible thyroid disease. If you live in a wooded area, or the dog is walked in such an area, be alert for ticks on his coat.

EYE CARE

Your Husky's vision also may deteriorate with age. A bluish haze is common in geriatric dogs and does not impair vision, but you should always check with your vet about any changes in the eyes to determine if it's harmless or a problem.

BENEATH THE SICKLE

How about his other end...does he chew at his rear or scoot and rub it on the carpet? That's a sign of impacted anal glands. Have your vet express those glands. Have annual stool cultures done to check for

Very young pups will be examined by a vet and started on their shots before they leave the breeder. The breeder should provide new owners with the relevant health documentation concerning their puppy.

intestinal parasites, which can cause weight and appetite loss, poor coat quality and intestinal problems, and weaken your dog's resistance. See your vet if any of those signs appear. Tapeworms, a common parasite, look like grains of rice in the stool.

HEART AND KIDNEY DISEASE

Heart disease is common in all canines, yet it is one that dog owners most frequently overlook. Symptoms include panting and shortness of breath, chronic coughing, especially at night or upon first waking in the morning, and changes in sleeping habits. Heart disease can be treated if you catch it early.

Kidney disease also can be treated successfully with early diagnosis. If your dog drinks excessive amounts of water and urinates more frequently, has accidents in the house, run, don't walk, to your vet. Kidney failure can be managed.

The lesson here is...know your dog. Early detection is the key to your dog's longevity and quality of life.

EMERGENCIES

Every dog owner should know the signs of an emergency. Many dog agencies, humane societies and animal shelters sponsor canine first-aid seminars.

Obvious emergencies include vomiting for more than 24 hours, bloody or prolonged (over 24 hours) diarrhea, fever (normal canine temperature is 101.5°F), and a sudden swelling of the head or any body part. Symptoms of other common emergency situations include:

Heatstroke—excessive panting, drooling, rapid pulse, dark reddened gums and a frantic, glazed expression.

Hypothermia—shivering, very pale gums and body temperature under 100°F.

Shock—severe blood loss from an injury can send a dog into shock. Symptoms include shivering, weak pulse, weakness and listlessness, depression and lowered body temperature.

Other symptoms that can be red flags for cancer or

other serious health problems include: lumps or abnormal swelling; sores that do not heal; sudden or unexplainable weight loss; loss of appetite, unexplained bleeding or discharge; an offensive body odor; difficulty swallowing or eating; loss of stamina or reluctance to exercise; difficulty breathing, urinating or defecating; a bloated appearance, persistent stiffness or lameness.

Call your veterinarian at once if you notice any of these warning signs. Many canine diseases and some cancers are treatable if they are diagnosed in the early stages.

Cultivate a keen awareness of even subtle changes in your dog. Make a list of any minor changes and the date you observed them. Read books on canine health care and first aid and add one to your library. Keep a list of symptoms and remedies in a handy place to reference when necessary. Your Husky's life could depend on it.

HOME CARE FOR YOUR HUSKY

Overview

- Body weight and the teeth are the two most important considerations in your Husky's home-care routine. Obesity and poor dental hygiene can threaten your dog's health and shorten his life.
- When grooming your Husky, watch for moles, bumps, lumps and parasites.
- From the Husky's eyes to the tip of his tail, the owner must inspect for signs of problems.
- Recognize your Husky's signs of wellness so that you know when the dog's health may be in jeopardy.

Feeding Your Siberian Husky

The Siberian Husky is considered an "easy keeper" that requires less food than most breeds its size. Breed experts speculate that this trait dates back to the Husky's original breeders, the Chukchis, who developed their dogs to pull lightweight sleds in extreme cold, traveling great distances on a minimal amount of food.

However, the quality of the Husky's food is an extremely important concern. Premium dog-food manufacturers have developed their formulas with strict quality controls to provide balanced and complete nutrition. Do

The breeder starts the litter out on a good solid food, and you should take his advice as to how to continue feeding once your puppy comes home with you.

not add your own supplements, "people food" or extra vitamins to the food. You will only offset the nutritional balance of the food, which could affect the growth pattern and overall maintenance of your Husky.

Huskies generally have good appetites and will dive into mealtimes with both feet.

The major dog-food brands now offer foods for every breed, age and activity level. Make sure that you select a high-quality food for your Siberian Husky that is based on animal protein. A protein content of no less than 26% and a fat content of no less than 18% are required for Huskies of all ages. There is no need to change the dog's diet once you establish him on a suitable food. Remember to avoid soy products in your Husky's food.

The active Husky needs proper nutrition to stay in peak condition. Do your research and only feed a top-quality food that contains the correct percentage of protein and fat.

Ask your breeder and your vet which food they recommend for your Husky pup. A solid education about dog food will provide the tools you need to offer your dog a diet that is best for early growth as well as long-term health. You are best to continue feeding the premium brand that the breeder uses. He knows his dogs and their needs. If, however, you plan to feed something other than the

Your Husky's attitude will change when there's a treat at stake. Never underestimate the power of food when trying to persuade your dog, but also be careful not to overdo it with the tidbits.

breeder's food, take home a small supply of that food to mix with your own to aid your puppy's adjustment to his new food.

When and how much to

feed? An eight-week-old puppy does best eating three times a day—tiny tummies, tiny meals. At about 12 weeks of age, you can switch to twice-daily feeding. Most breeders suggest two meals a day for the life of the dog, regardless of breed.

Free-feeding, that is, leaving a bowl of food available all day, is not recommended. Free-feeding fosters picky eating habits. Free-feeders are also more likely to become possessive of their food bowls.

An advantage to the two-meal-a-day plan is that it's easier to predict elimination, which is the better road to house-training. Regular meals also help you know just how much your puppy eats and when, valuable information if your pup gets sick.

Like people, puppies and adult dogs have different appetites. It's easy to

overfeed a chow hound.
Who can resist those exotic
Husky eyes? You should!
Chubby puppies may be cute
and cuddly, but the extra
weight will stress his
growing joints and is thought
to be a factor in the development of hip disease.
Overweight pups also tend to
grow into overweight adults
who tire easily and will be
more susceptible to other
health problems. So always
remember that lean is
healthy, fat is not. Obesity is
a major canine killer.

Should you feed canned
or dry food? Dry food is
recommended by most vets,
since the dry particles help
clean the dog's teeth of
plaque and tartar. Adding
water to dry food is optional,
though it can stimulate the
dog's appetite. The food hog
who almost inhales his food
may do better with a splash
of water in his food pan.
Whether feeding wet or dry,
always have clean, fresh
water available.

FEEDING YOUR SIBERIAN HUSKY

Overview

- Compared to other working breeds, the Husky requires consid-
erably less food. This trait is associated with the dog's Chukchi
sled-dog origins.
- Feed the best-quality food based on animal protein to your Husky.
Never compromise by purchasing second-rate dog food as the quality
of the food affects the dog's coat, overall health and behavior.
- Your breeder (and/or vet) can advise you about the proper amount to
feed your Husky.
- Schedule two daily feedings for an adult dog.
- Avoid overfeeding with your Husky, as obesity can lead to other health
problems in your dog.

CHAPTER 12

Grooming Your Siberian Husky

Good grooming habits, involve much more than coat care. It also includes your Husky's skin, teeth, ears and nails, and is a safety check for abnormalities that can hide beneath your dog's fur coat. And let's not forget the bonding benefits of hands-on attention from his human.

Every dog should enjoy the grooming process; it's the next best thing to petting. The brush, nail clippers and toothbrush are best introduced when your Husky is just a pup. Some older dogs who have not experienced these

Introduce your puppy to the brush, using soft strokes, a gentle touch and soothing words.

ministrations may object when they are older...and bigger...and better able to resist. The moral here...start young.

Start with tiny increments of time, stroking him gently with a soft brush, briefly handling his paws, looking inside his ears, gently touching his gums. Offer little dog treats during each session.

Your Husky's coat can pick up all sorts of unwanted guests outdoors: insects, burrs, grasses and the like. Thorough checks of his skin and coat are important during your grooming sessions and after time spent outdoors.

The Siberian Husky carries a double coat, medium in length. The coat is relatively odor-free and not highly allergenic. Huskies shed their undercoat twice a year, usually in late spring and again in fall. Extensive bathing and brushing during those periods are necessary to remove the excess fur. If you are a fussy house-keeper, think twice about adding a Husky to your household.

How often should you bathe your Husky? In most cases, no more than once every month or two, except during shedding season, and less

The adult Husky is most heavily coated around his chest and neck; a protective mane designed to insulate his heart, lungs and other vital organs.

often if your dog stays out of mud holes! Too frequent bathing will remove those essential oils that keep your dog's skin supple and his coat soft and gleaming.

But of course there are those times when a bath is necessary. To minimize the stress and struggle of bath time, start when your pup is small. Lure your puppy into the tub with a food reward. Line the tub or shower with a

While it is necessary to clean your Husky's ears, it is not advised to poke into the ears with a swab or anything else. A soft cotton pad or ball is safer to clean the outer ears.

towel for safe footing. Start with a dry tub and gradually add shallow water and the bathing process. After shampooing, always be sure to rinse the coat completely to avoid any itching from residual shampoo. A good chamois is the ideal tool for drying as it absorbs water like a sponge. Hair dryers designed for dogs are especially handy for drying heavy-coated breeds like Huskies. Keep him away from drafts for a good while after bathing and drying to prevent chilling.

A daily tooth brushing is the ideal, but twice weekly may be more realistic. Use a doggie toothbrush or rub his teeth with a gauze pad or soft washcloth.

Nails should be trimmed once a month. Start nail clipping as soon as possible, since the longer you wait, the less he will cooperate. Puppies naturally do not like to have their nails trimmed.

Offer those puppy treats with each clipping lesson to create a positive association.

Nip off the nail tip or clip at the curved part of the nail. Be careful not to cut the quick (the pink vein in the nail), as that is quite painful, and the nail may bleed profusely. You can staunch the bleeding with a few drops of a clotting solution available from your veterinarian. Keep it on hand…accidents happen.

Weekly ear checks are worth the proverbial pound of cure. Although ear infections are common to all breeds of dogs, the Husky's prick ears are less prone to chronic ear infection than are the drop-eared breeds. Regular cleansing with a specially formulated ear cleanser will keep your dog's ears clean and odor-free.

Symptoms of ear infection include redness and/or swelling of the ear flap or inner ear, a nasty odor or dark, waxy discharge. If your dog digs at his ear(s) with his paw, holds his head to one side, shakes his head a lot, or appears to lose his balance, see your vet at once.

GROOMING YOUR SIBERIAN HUSKY

Overview

- The Husky's medium-length double coat requires regular grooming to keep looking its absolute best.
- Huskies shed, especially during their season coat changes, when daily grooming is called for.
- Occasional baths keep the Husky's coat clean.
- Owners must tend to the Husky's teeth twice a week, his ears once a week and his nails once a month.
- Ear problems can escalate in no time at all, so attend to a possible infection as soon as you notice one.

Keeping the Husky Active

When discussing Siberian Husky activity, the key word is "busy." Classified in the AKC Working Group of dogs, the Siberian was bred to run, and run he will at every opportunity. The Husky needs a minimum of one hour of vigorous exercise each day.

More than just a healthy habit, exercise and physical activity are essential to your Husky's mental health as well as his physical well-being. A well-exercised Husky is happily tired and less inclined to find mischievous outlets

Bright, intelligent dogs like the Siberian Husky need daily stimulation of mind and body. Keep him busy and happy.

for his unexpended energy. Although all canines benefit from some form of daily exercise, the Husky needs something to do. Almost a century ago his primary function was that of an endurance sled dog. The modern Husky still hears the same ancestral call and needs challenging activity to channel his Husky energy.

Given the chance to explore, the Husky will be off and running, impressing all with his agility and athleticism.

That said, bear in mind that neither the Husky puppy nor adult will get proper exercise on his own. Left to his own devices, the Husky will dig or chew relentlessly out of sheer boredom. A long, brisk on-leash daily walk, even two, will help keep your Husky fit and trim, as well as keep his mind stimulated through the sights and sounds of street life or the neighborhood park.

Obedience and agility events provide excitement, exercise and entertainment to dog and owner alike.

How long and how far to walk depends on your Husky's age, his physical condition and energy level. A young Husky's bones are soft and more vulnerable to injury during his first year of life and should not be subjected to heavy stress. That means shorter, more frequent walks, no games that encourage high jumping or heavy impact on his front or rear until your pup is past the danger age.

When and where to walk is as important as how long. On warm days, avoid walking during midday heat and go out during the cooler morning or evening hours. If you're a jogger, your Husky buddy is the perfect running companion. Just make sure your buddy is in good condition and up to doing your mile-plus run,

Those daily walks are also excellent bonding sessions. Your Husky will look forward to his special time with you. As a creature of habit, your dog will bounce with joy when he sees you don your cap, pick up his leash, or rattle your keys.

Consider taking your

exercise program to another level. Plan a weekly night out with your Husky and enroll in a dog class. Obedience, maybe agility…or both. You will be motivated to work with your dog daily so you don't look unprepared or unraveled at each week's class. You'll both be more active, and thus healthier. Your dog will learn the basics of obedience, will be better behaved and will become a model citizen.

Agility class offers even more healthy outlets for Husky energy. He will learn to scale an A-frame ramp, race headlong through a tunnel, balance himself on a teeter-totter, jump up and off a platform, jump through a hoop and zig-zag between a line of posts. The challenge of learning to navigate these agility obstacles, and his success in mastering each one, will make you proud of both of you!

You can take both of these activities one step further and

show your dog in obedience and agility competition. Find a club or join a training group. Working with other fanciers will give you the incentive to keep working with your dog. Check the Siberian Husky Club of America (SHCA) and AKC websites for details.

Conformation dog showing is by far the most popular canine competition for all breeds. If you plan to show your Husky, make sure you look for a show-quality puppy and discuss your goals with the breeder. Most local breed clubs host conformation training classes and can help novices get started with their pups.

The SHCA offers more opportunities for your Husky to have a great time pursuing his pulling heritage. The SHCA Working Programs sponsor sled-dog events to promote and preserve the pulling instincts of the Siberian Husky. You may also want to investigate weight-pulling competitions for your Husky. These are sponsored by the International Weight Pull Association (IWPA).

KEEPING THE HUSKY ACTIVE

Overview

- A working dog like the Husky needs plenty of daily exercise. Keep your Husky busy for a couple of hours per day.
- Exercise should include at least two daily walks and free running time in a safely enclosed area.
- Puppies should be exercised less than adult dogs.
- Limit activity on warm days—this is a Nordic breed that prefers the cold and snow to the sun and humidity.
- Expand your exercise regimen to include agility and obedience lessons, or possibly trials. Consider dog shows, weight pulls and instinct tests to keep your Husky active and happy.

CHAPTER 14

Your Husky and His Vet

T ake your pup to his veterinarian within three or four days after he comes home. Show the vet any health records of shots and wormings from your breeder. The vet will conduct a thorough physical exam to make sure your pup is in good health, and work out a schedule for vaccinations, routine medications and regular well-puppy visits.

VACCINES

Vaccine protocol varies with many veterinarians. The vaccines most commonly recommended by the America Veterinary Medical Association (AVMA). These include:

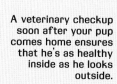

A veterinary checkup soon after your pup comes home ensures that he's as healthy inside as he looks outside.

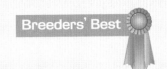
distemper, canine parvovirus, canine adenovirus, canine hepatitis and rabies.

Vaccines no longer routinely recommended by the AVMA, except when the risk is present, are canine parainfluenza, leptospirosis, canine coronavirus, Bordetella (canine cough) and Lyme (borreliosis). These diseases are not considered fatal or overly risky.

Rabies vaccination is mandatory in all 50 states. For many years the rabies vaccine has been available in a one-year and a three-year vaccine. Check with your state to find out if the three-year vaccine is legal in your state.

Your vet will pick up where the breeder left off with vaccinations. Take his advice and be sure to follow up with booster shots as needed.

HEARTWORM

This is a worm that propagates inside your dog's heart and will ultimately kill your dog. Now found in all 50 states, heartworm is transmitted through a mosquito bite. Heartworm preventatives can be given daily or monthly in pill form or in a shot

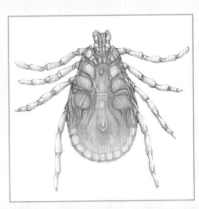

Ticks are common in rural areas and can carry various diseases.

Siberian Husky

Blue eyes in the Husky are certainly striking, especially when against darker coat. Also notice the abundance of protective hair lining the ears.

flea weapons to aid you in your battle against the pesky flea. Your vet can tell you about the most up-to-date advances. Over-the-counter flea and tick collars offer only limited protection.

Lyme's disease (canine borreliosis), Ehrlichiosis and Rocky Mountain spotted fever are tick-borne diseases now found in almost every state. These diseases can affect humans as well as dogs. Dogs that live in or visit areas where ticks are present, whether seasonally or year 'round, must be protected.

A well-informed dog owner is better prepared to raise a healthy dog. Always ask your vet what shots or medications your dog is getting and what they are for. Keep a notebook or dog diary and record all health information so you won't forget it. Believe me, you will forget.

Fortunately today's

given every six months, available only through your veterinarian. Depending on where you live, the necessity of heartworm preventatives varies.

FLEAS AND TICKS

Fortunately, today there are several low-toxic, effective

veterinary community is focused on preventative care and canine wellness as well as treating animals after they are sick. The American Holistic Veterinary Medical Association and other specialty groups now offer acupuncture, herbal remedies, homeopathy and other alternative therapies in addition to traditional disease treatment and prevention. Many pet owners today incorporate both philosophies in their dog's health-care programs. You can learn more about these alternative natural care disciplines through books or on the Internet.

REGULAR EXAMS

Well-dog examinations are the foundation of preventative health care, and your Husky should visit his veterinarian annually. Most importantly, an annual visit keeps your vet apprised of your pet's health progress,

and the hands-on exam often turns up small or internal abnormalities you can't see or feel.

Your Husky's health is in your hands between those annual visits to the vet. Be ever conscious of any changes in his appearance or behavior.

Has your Husky gained a few too many pounds or suddenly lost weight? Are his teeth clean and white or does he need some plaque attackers? Is he urinating more frequently, drinking more water than usual? Does he strain during a bowel movement? Are there any changes in his appetite? Does he appear short of breath, lethargic, overly tired? Have you noticed limping or signs of joint stiffness? These are all signs of serious health problems that you should discuss with your vet as soon as they appear. This is especially important for the senior dog, since even subtle changes can be a sign of something serious.

SPAYING/NEUTERING?

This is almost a non-question, since spaying/ neutering is the best health insurance policy you can give your Husky. Statistics prove that females spayed before their first heat cycle (estrus) have a 90% less risk of several common female cancers and other serious female health problems. Males neutered before their male hormones kick in, usually before six months of age, enjoy zero to greatly reduced risk of testicular and prostate cancer and other related tumors and infections. Additionally, males will be less apt to display those overt male behaviors that can be so frustrating for owners.

YOUR HUSKY AND HIS VET

Overview

- A visit to the veterinarian will be on top of your list of things to do with your new Siberian Husky puppy.
- The vet will set up a vaccination schedule for your dog. Keep records of all vaccines administered.
- Discuss a heartworm preventative program with your vet. Such a program may be required if you live in a rural area.
- Pesky parasites are the bane of every dog owner's existence, and dogs don't like them either. Discuss prevention and control with your vet.
- Annual visits with your Husky help ensure his long life.
- Spay or neuter your pet Husky at an appropriately young age, usually around six months.